Quick & Easy Internet Activities
for the One-Computer Classroom

Weather

by Mary Kay Carson

20 Fun, Web-based Activities With Reproducible
Graphic Organizers That Enable Kids to Learn the
Very Latest Information—On Their Own!

SCHOLASTIC
PROFESSIONAL BOOKS

New York • Toronto • London • Auckland • Sydney
Mexico City • New Delhi • Hong Kong • Buenos Aires

Cover design by **Norma Ortiz**

Interior design by **Holly Grundon**

Interior illustrations by **Ivy Rutzky**

ISBN: 0-439-27856-2

Copyright © 2002 by Mary Kay Carson

Contents

Using This Book

Welcome to *Quick & Easy Internet Activities for the One-Computer Classroom: Weather!* The 20 activities in this book will expand your students' knowledge of weather and build their Internet skills at the same time. The World Wide Web is a great resource for teaching a unit on weather. Where else can you get up-to-the-minute forecasts, radar images, and weather maps 24 hours a day, 7 days a week? The data and information available on the Web allow students to track storms and map fronts in real time.

What's Inside

This book is divided into four chapters: Sun, Air, & Wind; Water Cycle & Precipitation; Weather Watching & Forecasting; and Stormy Weather. Each of the 20 activities in this book comes with a teacher page, filled with background information, step-by-step mini-lessons, and extension activities. Reproducible student pages provide simple directions, graphic organizers, and recording sheets that help students complete Web-based activities, from simple scavenger hunts to projects that involve higher-level critical thinking. On page 7, you'll find a reproducible assessment sheet that you can use to evaluate students' projects.

Accessing the Web Sites

In the fast-paced world of the Web, sites can come and go quickly. In addition, some URLs (Uniform Resource Locations, or site addresses) are so long and unwieldy, students can accidentally type in the wrong address. For these reasons, we decided not to list specific URLs for the activities in this book. Instead, we have published all the necessary links on our own Web site.

To access the Web sites for this book, go to:

www.scholastic.com/profbooks/ netexplorations/index.htm

This address also appears at the top of the teacher and student pages. Click on the book cover for *Weather*. Remember to bookmark this site or add it to your favorites. Then, click on the links under each activity name to access the Web sites needed to complete the activity.

NOTE: You may want to check out the Web sites yourself before using them in your classroom. By becoming familiar with their content and organization, you'll be able to help students navigate through them more efficiently.

Tips for Managing Web-based Activities

The activities in this book are designed so that students can do much of the work away from the computer. Whether you have only one computer in your classroom or have access to a computer lab, here are some tips for helping students effectively manage their limited time on the computer:

Taking Turns

Assign each student or small group about 15 minutes of computer time in rotation. (Most of the activities in this book can be done by students in small groups.) Have the rest of the class complete the non-computer part of the activity, or give them related activities to do while waiting for their turn at the computer.

Focusing on the Task

Before students go to the computer, have them read their worksheets carefully so that they have a clear, focused objective of what to look for. When they go online, tell students that they don't need to read everything on a site—they can just browse for the information they need and jot it down on their worksheets.

Hooking Up a Projector

You can hook up your computer to a video monitor or a projector, and have your whole class browse the Web together. Students can participate by taking turns clicking on the hyperlinks or reading the information.

Using Offline Software

If you can't access the Internet in your classroom, try offline software, such as Web Whacker **(www.bluesquirrel.com)**, to capture all the pages in a Web site and download them. Students can then view the Web site from computers that aren't hooked to the Internet. You can also save Web pages as viewable documents and/or print them out, but they will likely not include pictures and graphics.

More Tips for Smooth Surfing

★ Review with students the basics of using their Internet browsers, such as typing in exact URLs, scrolling, going back and forward between Web pages, using hyperlinks, printing, and copying and pasting images.
★ Consider creating "Browser Basics" help sheets or index cards and posting them near the computer.
★ Many Web sites contain a barrage of information. Encourage students to browse the Web sites for the information they need, rather than read everything.

Evaluating Internet Sources

The Internet is a great research tool for both you and your students. The Web sites used in this book have been selected for their accuracy and age-appropriateness. But how will you know if information found in other sites is accurate? Here are some tips:

Where is it coming from?
Is the page sponsored by a trustworthy source, such as a government office, non-profit organization, or university? Read the "About This Site" link to find out.

Who wrote it?
Is an author given for the site? Are his or her qualifications stated? Is there information on how to contact the author?

How accurate is the information?
Are sources for the information provided or cited? Does it seem outdated or not very exact? Is there a publishing and/or a last-updated date? Does it look "professional"—free of spelling errors and typos?

What's the angle?
Is the information trying too hard to persuade you, or is it presented in an even-handed manner? Are there advertisements on the site? Whether the information is provided as an educational or public service or as a venue for promoting a product can make a difference in its content and objectivity. Sticking to Web sites with URLs that end in **.gov**, **.edu**, and **.org** is often safer, though still not foolproof.

Be choosy!
If the Web site and/or information seems suspect, it very likely is! If you can't corroborate a fact found on the Web site with any other source, it's probably not true.

Meeting the Science Standards

The lessons in this book meet many of the National Science Education Content Standards:

Unifying Concepts and Processes
★ Evidence, models, and explanation
★ Change, constancy, and measurement

Grades K–4
★ Objects in the sky
★ Changes in earth and sky
★ Science and technology in local challenges

Grades 5–8
★ Structure of the earth system
★ Earth in the solar system
★ Natural hazards
★ Science as a human endeavor

Project Evaluation Form

NAME: _____ DATE: _____

PROJECT: _____

Score

	Poor				Excellent
Follows Directions	1	2	3	4	5
Collaborates With Other Students *(cooperation, flexibility)*	1	2	3	4	5
Uses Computer Time Effectively *(goal-oriented, navigation skills)*	1	2	3	4	5
Curriculum Content *(research, organization, creativity)*	1	2	3	4	5
Writing *(clarity, organization, spelling, grammar)*	1	2	3	4	5
Supporting Visuals *(if applicable)*	1	2	3	4	5

TOTAL SCORE _____

Comments:

_____

_____

_____

_____

Science
Math

Where Weather Happens

Students learn about the atmosphere and create a large, to-scale poster of its layers.

BACKGROUND

Earth is surrounded by a thin blanket of gases called the *atmosphere*. Scientists divide the atmosphere into four or five main layers. The layer nearest the surface is the *troposphere*, where most weather happens. It has the most air and moisture. The *stratosphere* is the next layer, followed by the *mesosphere*. The *thermosphere* is the outermost true atmospheric layer, with interplanetary space (the *exosphere*) lying beyond.

DOING THE ACTIVITY

1. Engage students in a discussion about the air around them. Ask, Is there air out in space? *(No)* Is there as much air on top of Mt. Everest as down here? *(No)* How far out do you think there is air?

2. Divide the class into small groups. Photocopy and distribute page 9. Have students use the links at the above Web site to fill in information about each layer of the atmosphere, including its height. Students may need a kilometer-to-mile conversion chart or formula (kilometers x 0.6 = miles).

3. Have each group plan a poster of the atmosphere's layers using the information they collect. They need to convert the heights to a scale they can use, depending on how much space they'll have. (A scale of 1 km = 1 cm needs about 3 meters of wall space, for example.)

4. Provide students with yardsticks as well as art materials to create their posters. Have them label their posters with the names of the layers, their heights, and interesting facts about each layer.

More To Do:

How High Does It Fly?

Challenge students to find out at what height airplanes, kites, jets, weather balloons, and the space shuttle fly. Invite them to include drawings or cutout pictures of each craft on their posters or wall charts.

Name(s) _____   Date _____

GO TO: www.scholastic.com/profbooks/netexplorations/index.htm

The Earth's Atmosphere

Learn about the layers of the atmosphere using the links at the above Web site. Record the height of the topmost part of each layer in Chart A. In the last column, decide which unit of measurement you'll use to show each layer's height in your poster of the atmosphere. Then, in Chart B, take notes on each of the layers.

Chart A

	Height in kilometers	Height in miles	Height for poster with units
Thermosphere			
Mesosphere			
Stratosphere			
Troposphere	12	7	(Circle one.) 7 cm 7 in 12 cm 12 in

Chart B   **Cool Facts About Each Layer**

Thermosphere	
Mesosphere	
Stratosphere	
Troposphere	

Science
Geography
Critical
Thinking

All About Fronts

Students investigate three types of fronts and the weather they cause.

BACKGROUND

The boundary where two different air masses collide is called a *front*. It's a battleground of weather, where one air mass advances while another retreats. Often, the result is storms and other weather changes. If warm air is advancing, it's called a *warm front*. If cold air is pushing on the boundary, it's a *cold front*. A *stationary front* occurs when neither air mass is advancing.

DOING THE ACTIVITY

1. Photocopy and distribute page 11 to students. Point out the information about each front.

2. Show students a weather map that displays fronts from a newspaper or the Internet. Engage students in a discussion about weather fronts to help you assess what they already know and to prepare them for the activity.

3. Have students follow the directions on the worksheet. To save time, print out a map from the MAP links at the above Web site beforehand. Students will need access to a map that shows U.S. cities.

4. When students have finished, invite them to share their findings with the class and discuss the questions on the page.

ANSWERS

1. West **2.** Temperatures rise, and clouds and rain or snow often move in. **3.** Temperatures drop, and rain or snow and storms often follow.

More To Do:

Investigate Air

Investigate the types of air masses (continental, maritime, polar, and tropical) and the fronts they are generally associated with.

Name(s) _____   Date _____

Figuring Out Fronts

Print out a U.S. map that shows fronts from the MAP links at the above Web site. Read about the types of fronts below. Circle each front on your map that is over land. Label each COLD, WARM, or STATIONARY. Then fill out a mini-chart about each front below. Use the WEATHER links to find out the current weather in each city.

The **warm front** is a red line. The half circles point toward the direction the front is moving.

The **cold front** is a blue line. The triangles point toward the direction the front is moving.

The **stationary front** is a red and blue line.

Front Type: _____ Direction moving: _____
City behind front: _____
The weather there? _____
City ahead of front: _____
The weather there? _____

Front Type: _____ Direction moving: _____
City behind front: _____
The weather there? _____
City ahead of front: _____
The weather there? _____

Front Type: _____ Direction moving: _____
City behind front: _____
The weather there? _____
City ahead of front: _____
The weather there? _____

QUESTIONS:

1. Do fronts move mostly from the west or east?

_____

2. How do warm fronts change the weather as they pass over a city?

_____

_____

3. How do cold fronts change the weather as they pass over a city?

_____

_____

Science Social Studies

Watching the Wind

Students use the Beaufort scale to estimate winds at various Webcam sites and out their own window.

BACKGROUND

In 1805, a British naval admiral named Sir Francis Beaufort invented a wind-measuring scale that required no instruments. It was based on the effects wind has on the physical environment—in his case, what ocean waves and ship sails looked like. Wind strengths were divided into 13 categories called *forces*. The Beaufort scale was later adapted for land use and is still used today to estimate wind speeds.

DOING THE ACTIVITY

1. Introduce the term *anemometer* to students and, if possible, show them examples of wind-measuring instruments. Discuss how people may have measured wind before such instruments were invented, or what they do when instruments aren't available. Introduce the Beaufort scale.

2. Photocopy and distribute page 13 to students or student pairs. Have students visit the live Webcam sites (click on the above site for links) and fill out their charts. Note: The computer must be able to process "streaming video" to see the Webcam sites.

3. As a final step, invite students to record the local wind by looking out a window and noting the wind's effects on objects.

4. When students have finished, ask them to name the places that were the windiest. Have students compare the Beaufort scale ratings they gave the sites. Were their findings similar for identical sites?

More To Do:

Build an Anemometer

Tape one end of a 12-inch thread to a Ping-Pong ball and the other to the center of a protractor's base. Hold this "anemometer" level, with the protractor's base up, and make sure the ball swings freely. To measure the wind, stand facing into the wind and hold the anemometer away from you. The higher the ball is lifted, the stronger the wind.

Name(s) _____ Date _____

GO TO: www.scholastic.com/profbooks/netexplorations/index.htm

Where's It Windy?

Click on the links at the above Web site to print out the Beaufort scale. Then open a Webcam site (from the links). Note which town the camera targets on the chart under Webcam 1. Describe what the wind is like there. Are trees swaying or leaves blowing? Use the Beaufort scale to assign a force number to the wind's strength. Complete the rest of the chart by visiting other sites. The last block is for recording your local wind.

Webcam 1

Where? _____
_____

What's the wind doing? _____
_____
_____

Beaufort scale number: _____

Webcam 2

Where? _____
_____

What's the wind doing? _____
_____
_____

Beaufort scale number: _____

Webcam 3

Where? _____
_____

What's the wind doing? _____
_____
_____

Beaufort scale number: _____

Out the Window

Where are you?_____
_____

What's the wind doing? _____
_____
_____

Beaufort scale number: _____

Science
Geography

How Hot Is It There?

Students investigate the connection between latitude
and surface temperature by looking up the current temperature
at varying distances from the equator.

BACKGROUND

Sunlight heats land and water, and they in turn heat the air above them.
The air's temperature is a measure of the air molecules' speed—the
faster they're moving, the hotter they are. Earth's surface averages about
59°F at sea level. But our planet isn't evenly heated. Temperatures
around the world range from about –130°F to 140°F and depend on
the season, latitude, elevation, and time of day.

DOING THE ACTIVITY

1. Use a globe or map to begin your lesson and to start students thinking
   about temperature and latitude. Ask students to name places where it
   never snows and find those places on the map, noting their latitudes.
   Ask them to name places where it's always cold and find those places
   on the map, again noting their latitudes.

2. Photocopy and distribute page 15 to students. Have students use the
   links at the above Web site to find the current temperature for each
   city on the worksheet. Provide assistance if students need help finding
   the cities. Make sure students include units with each temperature.

3. When students have finished, discuss the findings as a class. Ask,
   Where was it coldest? Hottest? Is there a pattern? *(Temperatures are
   warmer closer to the equator.)* Why? *(The sun's light and energy hits the equator
   straight on with full strength. Farther from the equator, the sun's angle is less
   direct and its energy less concentrated.)*

More To Do:

Graph It

Invite students to use their results to graph temperature versus latitude.
They'll need to first look up the latitude of each city using an atlas or map.

GO TO: www.scholastic.com/profbooks/netexplorations/index.htm

Mapping Out Temperature

Use the links at the above Web site to find the current temperature for the eight cities on the map below. Write the temperature, with units (Fahrenheit or Celsius), in the box near each city's name.

Think: Is there a pattern to the temperatures? What is it?

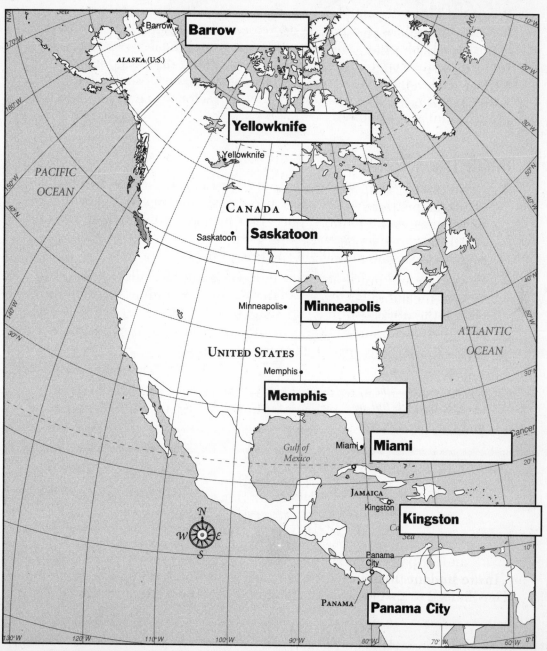

Science
Health
Language
Arts

The Air We Breathe

Students learn about factors that contribute to air quality, record the pollution, pollen, and UV radiation levels for a city, and then write a report for that city.

BACKGROUND

Pollutants such as ground-level ozone (smog), carbon monoxide, nitrogen dioxide, lead, and sulfur dioxide decrease the quality of the air we breathe. Significant levels of air pollution affect everyone's health, especially the very young, the very old, and those with breathing disorders, such as asthma. Pollen and mold spores also reduce air quality for allergy sufferers. Sunlight strength (UV radiation) is another factor that needs to be taken into account when outdoors.

DOING THE ACTIVITY

1. Ask students, Do you have allergies or asthma? Are there months or seasons when you have more problems? Do you ever check the weather for an air-quality report? Explain that air quality and UV radiation are often part of weather reports. These reports help people make decisions about spending time outside.

2. Photocopy and distribute page 17 to each student. Allow students to choose a major U.S. city, or assign one to each student. If students can't locate their city on a U.S. map, provide a reference map.

3. Have students browse the links at the above Web site to complete their reports. Students will likely need to visit a number of Web sites to complete each topic.

4. Instruct students to write a report (or alert, if warranted) for the weather segment of a radio news show on the back of their paper.

More To Do:

Pollution Posters

Invite student pairs to create posters that illustrate everyday ways we can all help to reduce air pollution, such as riding a bike or walking instead of driving, conserving energy by turning off lights, or not having clothes dry-cleaned.

Name(s) _____   Date _____

GO TO: www.scholastic.com/profbooks/netexplorations/index.htm

How Healthy Is it Outside?

Browse links at the above Web site to find out how air pollution, pollen, and sunlight can harm your health. Then choose a U.S. city to report on and write its name below. Use the Web sites to fill out the report. Then write a radio script of your findings on the back of this page.

Report for _____
(city, state)

Air Pollution
Air Quality Index (circle one):   good   moderate   unhealthy   very unhealthy

Who might be affected and how? _____

What should people do to stay safe? _____

Allergies/Asthma
Pollen Count (circle one):   low   moderate   high

Who might be affected and how? _____

What should people do to stay safe? _____

Sun Exposure (UV Radiation)
Ultraviolet (UV) Index (circle one):   minimal   low   moderate   high   very high

Who might be affected and how? _____

What should people do to stay safe? _____

Is this report an ALERT? _____   **If so, for whom?** _____

Science Language Arts

Water Go-Round

Students learn about the water cycle and write the life story of a drop of water.

BACKGROUND

The continual movement of water between Earth's surface and the atmosphere is called the *water cycle. Precipitation* falls from clouds and forms lakes and rivers. Water on land *evaporates* into the air as does water *transpired* through plant leaves. Water vapor in the air *condenses* into clouds and eventually forms precipitation. Water changes phases between liquid, gas, and sometimes solid, as it moves through the water cycle.

DOING THE ACTIVITY

1. Introduce the water cycle to students. Ask, Where does rain come from? *(Clouds)* Where do clouds come from? *(Water vapor in the air)* Where does water in the air come from? *(Water evaporated from land and through plants)* Where does water on land come from? *(Rain)* Consider reviewing the different phases of water.

2. Photocopy and distribute page 19 to each student. Have students browse the links at the above Web site to label their water cycle diagrams and take notes.

3. When students have finished, have them write their stories away from the computer. Note: Consider discussing students' findings as a class to check their understanding before they write their stories.

ANSWERS

1. transpiration 2. condensation 3. precipitation 4. evaporation

---

More To Do:

- - - - - - - - - - - - - - - - - - - -

Observing Transpiration

Students can observe transpiration by placing plastic bags around houseplants and observing the water droplets that form on the leaves.

Name(s) _____   Date _____

The Life of Water

Water is always on the move. Click on the links at the above Web site to find out how water changes as it moves from sky to land and back to the sky. Label the blanks on the diagram with one of these words: EVAPORATION, CONDENSATION, TRANSPIRATION, and PRECIPITATION. Write some notes about each stage below the label. Then write the life story of a drop of water on the back of this page. In the story, include when the water is liquid, solid, or gas.

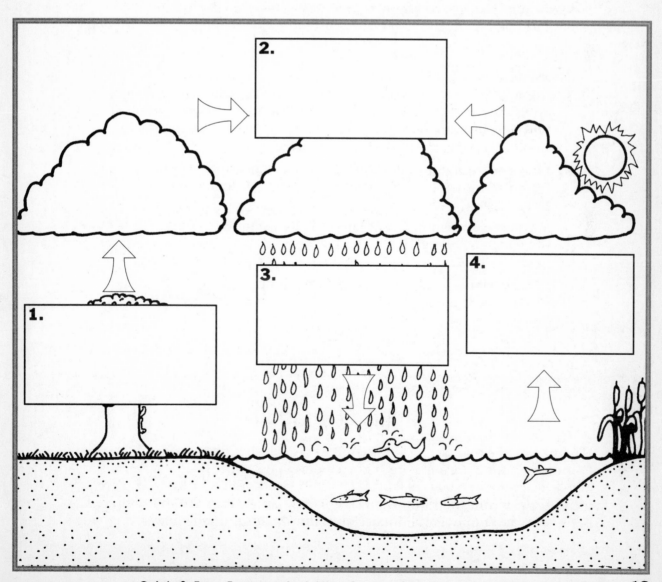

Science
Art

Meet-the-Clouds Mobile

Students learn about the different kinds of clouds, and then create a cloud mobile.

BACKGROUND

Clouds are made up of tiny water droplets and/or ice crystals suspended by air and updrafts. Clouds are classified into many identifiable types. Each cloud looks different because it is formed by variable mixes of ice, water, and wind. *Cirrus* clouds are white, for example, because they form at such a high altitude that all their water is in the form of ice crystals that scatter sunlight and appear white. *Cumulonimbus* clouds are dark because their abundant liquid-water droplets block sunlight.

DOING THE ACTIVITY

1. Ask students to name as many kinds of clouds as they can. Write them on the board. Ask, How are these clouds different from each other? Why? Remind students that clouds exist at different altitudes and are made of varying amounts of water and ice.

2. Photocopy and distribute page 21 to each student pair or small group. Tell students that they'll be making a mobile of cloud types.

3. Have students click on the links at the above Web site to collect information about different kinds of clouds on their chart.

4. Provide students with hangers, scissors, yarn, tape, cotton balls, glue, index cards, and watercolor paints to create their cloud mobiles. Invite students to label the backs of the index cards with the cloud names and to hang them from the hanger according to altitude.

More To Do:

Translate Clouds

The names of clouds are made up of Latin words that describe their shape and often their altitude. *Cirro-* means high, a cloud that's above 20,000 feet. *Alto-* means mid-level, or about 6,000–20,000 feet. (There is no prefix for low.) The prefix or suffix *-nimbo-* means the cloud is making precipitation. Invite students to use these Latin word roots to translate their clouds into "plain English" descriptive names.

Name(s) _____ Date _____

GO TO: www.scholastic.com/profbooks/netexplorations/index.htm

Chart the Clouds

Fill in the chart with names and facts about different kinds of clouds. (The first one has been done for you.) Then use index cards, cotton, and glue to create the clouds and assemble them into a mobile.

Cloud Name	Height	Color	Shape	Draw It!
Cirrus	upper-level 5,000-13,000 meters	white	thin, wispy strands	

**Science
Language
Arts**

Sorting Out Precipitation

**Students compare and contrast different types of precipitation
and then write TV quiz show-style questions about them.**

BACKGROUND

The type of precipitation that falls from a cloud depends on the cloud's
size and temperature, and the temperature of the air on the way down.
Drizzle is made up of small water drops, while *raindrops* are larger. *Freezing
rain* falls as water and freezes into ice on contact with any surface, while
sleet is made up of raindrops that have frozen in midair. *Snow* is made
up of ice crystals. *Hailstones* are balls of ice created in thunderstorm
updrafts.

DOING THE ACTIVITY

1. Ask students to name as many kinds of precipitation as they can. Note
   that all precipitation falls from clouds. *Frost* and *dew* are not precipitation; neither is *fog*, which is a low-lying cloud. Reinforce this concept
   by asking students what all the different kinds of precipitation have in
   common. *(They are made of water and fall from clouds.)*

2. Photocopy and distribute page 23 to students or student pairs. Have
   students click on the links at the above Web site to fill in their graphic
   organizers.

3. Invite students to write their TV quiz show-style questions on index
   cards, giving the answers on back.

4. When students have written their questions, invite them to play a
   number of rounds of a TV quiz show-style game.

More To Do:

Precipitation Poems

The different kinds of precipitation make great poetry themes. Have each student
choose a type of precipitation and write a poem about such details as its shape, feel,
or effects. Invite students to illustrate their poems with rainy or snowy scenes.

Name(s) _____   Date _____

GO TO: www.scholastic.com/profbooks/netexplorations/index.htm

Sleet or Snow? Rain or Drizzle?

Use the links at the above Web site to gather information on six different kinds of precipitation. Then try to stump your classmates by writing TV quiz show questions about the various kinds of precipitation.

Rain How does it happen? _____ What kinds of clouds/storms bring it? _____	**Hail** How does it happen? _____ What kinds of clouds/storms bring it? _____
Sleet How does it happen? _____ What kinds of clouds/storms bring it? _____	**Freezing Rain** How does it happen? _____ What kinds of clouds/storms bring it? _____
Snow How does it happen? _____ What kinds of clouds/storms bring it? _____	**Drizzle** How does it happen? _____ What kinds of clouds/storms bring it? _____

Science
Art

Snowflake Science

Students investigate the connection between snow crystal shape and temperature, and then create paper snowflakes.

BACKGROUND

Snowflakes are ice crystals. Snow crystals are famous for their six-sided shape. This hexagonal organization comes from the way water molecules behave when they freeze. There are a variety of snowflake shapes, determined in part by the temperature. Colder temperatures bring classic snowflake shapes, whereas warmer temperatures create needle- and column-shaped crystals.

DOING THE ACTIVITY

1. Start a class discussion about the saying "No two snowflakes are ever alike." Is it true? Why do people say it? *(The saying isn't technically true, but it speaks to the great variety of snowflake shapes.)* Explain that different weather conditions create differently shaped snowflakes.

2. Photocopy and distribute page 25 to each student. Have students browse the links at the above Web site to fill in the chart with their snow crystal drawings.

3. Provide students with square pieces of paper and scissors and ask them to follow the instructions for creating paper snow crystals.

More To Do:

Frosty Crystals

Frost is made up of crystals of frozen water. A frost-covered glass can have amazing and beautiful patterns that students can observe with magnifying lenses. Quickly dip glass jars or glasses in water and put them in a freezer for about 10 minutes. Make sure students have their magnifying lenses and science journals before passing out the glasses. They won't stay frosty for long! Encourage students to sketch in their science journal the patterns they see and then compare shapes with classmates.

Making Snow

Check the links at the above Web site to find out how temperature helps shape a snowflake. Draw a snow crystal next to the thermometer for each temperature. Then follow the instructions below to create your own paper snowflake.

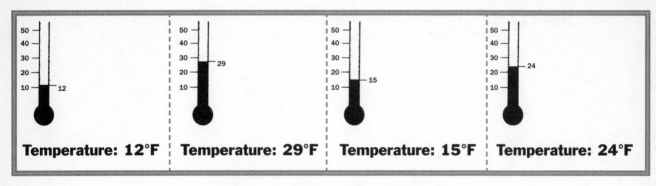

Temperature: 12°F | Temperature: 29°F | Temperature: 15°F | Temperature: 24°F

Fold-and-Cut Snowflake

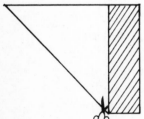

1. To form a square, fold a sheet of paper as shown and trim the excess.

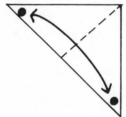

2. Fold the resulting triangle in half to make a smaller triangle.

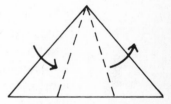

3. Next, fold the triangle in thirds—one section toward the front and the other to the back.

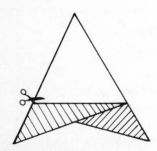

4. Trim off the excess again.

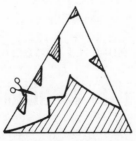

5. Now you're ready to cut! Cut snips and pieces out of the sides.

6. Unfold the paper to see your snowy creation!

Science
Language
Arts

Reporting the Weather

Students gather current weather information for a U.S. city and then write a weather report from the collected data.

BACKGROUND

More than 3,500 weather stations around the world take hourly measurements of temperature, air pressure, wind direction and speed, humidity, and other current weather readings. They then transmit these measurements to central weather forecasting and reporting centers. The weather station data is combined with data collected by aircraft, weather balloons, radar, and satellites to determine current weather conditions.

DOING THE ACTIVITY

1. Ask students what information is included in a weather report. *(Temperature, wind speed, humidity)* List each on the board. Check for understanding of each component as preparation for the activity.

2. Photocopy and distribute page 27 to each student. Assign a major U.S. city to each student, or allow them to choose their own.

3. Have students click on the links at the above Web site to fill in their data charts. Students will need to type in their chosen city and state to locate information on some Web sites. Make sure students understand that they are recording current conditions. Not all the Web sites have all the information, so students may need to visit multiple sites.

4. When students have completed their charts, have them write a weather report based on their data on the backs of their worksheets.

More To Do:

Today's Weather

Designate some wall space for a daily weather report. It can include the current temperature, humidity, cloud cover, air pressure, and wind speed and direction. Have students take turns filling in the information each day from local weather reports.

Name(s) _____   Date _____

GO TO: www.scholastic.com/profbooks/netexplorations/index.htm

Write a Weather Report

Browse the links at the above Web site to find the current weather conditions in your chosen city. Fill in the blanks below with the information you find. Then write a report of your chosen city's current weather on the back of this page.

Current Weather Conditions

City: _____

Date: _____   Local Time: _____

Temperature: _____ °F/°C (circle units)

Windchill Temperature: _____ °F/°C (circle units)

Relative Humidity: _____ %   Dew Point Temperature _____°F/°C (circle units)

Wind Speed: _____ mph/kph (circle units)

Wind Direction: _____

Cloud Cover: _____

Air Pressure/Barometer: _____ inches/millibars (circle units)

Science Math

Mapping the Weather I

Students decode a weather-station plot symbol to understand the weather information it holds.

BACKGROUND

A *surface weather map* shows the latest weather conditions. Its data comes from the thousands of weather stations around the world that record hourly weather measurements. Each station's information is presented in a *station plot,* a standardized symbol on a map that concisely conveys temperature, pressure, dew point temperature, wind direction and speed, cloud cover, and current weather conditions, like rain or snow.

DOING THE ACTIVITY

1. Print out a surface weather map for your region from a MAP Web site (click on the links at the above site) and show it to students. Ask them what they think all the small symbols and surrounding numbers represent. *(Station plots from weather stations)* Challenge them to identify the kind of weather represented by particular symbols on the map.

2. Photocopy and distribute page 29 to students. Have them browse the Web sites to label their station plot. Consider checking their work as a class or individually before they answer the questions at the bottom of the sheet or proceed to "Mapping the Weather II."

ANSWERS

1. 29°F **2.** 18°F **3.** NW **4.** 15 knots **5.** snowing **6.** light **7.** sea-level pressure in millibars **8.** overcast

More To Do:

Flashy Weather Symbols

Invite students to create flash cards of weather station plot symbols of weather, cloud cover, and wind barbs (wind speed and direction). They can draw the symbols or print them out from Web sites, and paste them onto cards.

Decode the Weather

The symbol below tells what the weather was like at the weather station in Buffalo, New York, on December 7. Using the links at the above Web site, decode this weather station plot by labeling its parts. (It's called a plot because it goes on a map.) Then answer the questions below.

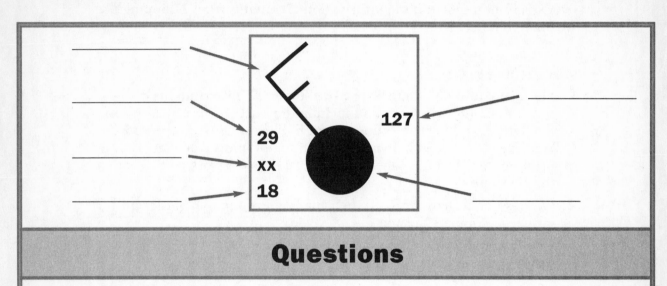

Questions

1. What is the air temperature? (include units) _____

2. What is the dew point temperature? (include units) _____

3. From which direction is the wind blowing? _____

4. What is the wind speed? (include units) _____

5. Is it raining or snowing? _____

6. Is the rain or snow light or heavy? _____

7. What does 127 represent? _____

8. How cloudy is it? _____

Science
Geography
Math

Mapping the Weather II

Students create a surface weather map by converting weather information into station plots and drawing them on a map.

BACKGROUND

Review a station plot and the information it contains from "Mapping the Weather I," if necessary.

DOING THE ACTIVITY

1. Photocopy and distribute page 31 to students. Have students draw a station plot for each city and include the weather information for that city from the chart. Students can browse the links at the above Web site if they need help creating the station plots. You can also print out the Web site pages to enable students to work away from the computer.

2. When students have finished their maps, allow them to gather in groups to compare answers.

ANSWERS

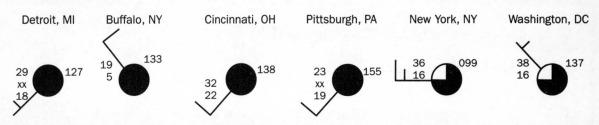

| Detroit, MI | Buffalo, NY | Cincinnati, OH | Pittsburgh, PA | New York, NY | Washington, DC |

More To Do:

All Sorts of Symbols

Have students look at examples of weather symbols on newspaper or television weather maps. Are they similar to or different from the station plot symbols? Divide the class into small groups and challenge each group to come up with their own symbols.

Name(s) _____   Date _____

GO TO: www.scholastic.com/profbooks/netexplorations/index.htm

Plot the Weather

Create a weather station plot for each of the six cities on the map, using the information in the chart below. Use the Web pages to help you create the correct symbols.

City	Air Temp.	Weather	Dew Point Temp.	Sea-Level Pressure	Wind Direction	Wind Speed	Cloud Cover
Detroit, MI	29°F	light snow	18°F	1012.7 mb	southwest	5 kts	overcast
Buffalo, NY	19°F	none	5°F	1013.3 mb	northwest	10 kts	overcast
Cincinnati, OH	32°F	none	22°F	1013.8 mb	southwest	10 kts	overcast
Pittsburgh, PA	23°F	light snow	19°F	1015.5 mb	southwest	10 kts	overcast
New York, NY	36°F	none	16°F	1009.9 mb	west	15 kts	broken clouds
Washington, DC	38°F	none	16°F	1013.7 mb	northwest	5 kts	broken clouds

Science Technology

High-Tech Weather Watch

Students investigate and compare real-time weather radar and satellite images.

BACKGROUND

Satellite images show clouds from above and can spot storms and hurricanes. Satellites also provide temperatures of the tops of clouds and the upper atmosphere, and the location of otherwise invisible water vapor. *Radar* shows the location and intensity of rain, snow, hail, or other precipitation. Radar works by sending out radio waves and analyzing their returning echoes. *Doppler radar* is a new and improved type of radar that not only measures precipitation, but also shows wind speed and direction.

DOING THE ACTIVITY

1. Discuss how weather information is measured and collected. Ask students to name as many weather-measuring instruments and tools as they can. Direct the discussion toward high-tech tools, such as computers, satellites, and radar. Use the discussion to assess what your students know about radar and satellite technology and how they are used in weather reporting and forecasting.

2. Photocopy and distribute page 33 to students or student pairs. Have students click on the links at the above Web site to browse both INFORMATION sites and MAP sites to fill in their charts. Students can complete their comparison charts at the computer, or they can print out a satellite and radar map and complete the chart away from the computer after browsing the INFORMATION Web sites.

3. Discuss the results as a class, if possible.

More To Do:

High-Tech History

Invite groups of students to research the history and development of satellite or radar technology and report on it.

Name(s) _____   Date _____

Satellite vs. Radar

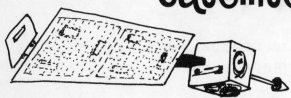
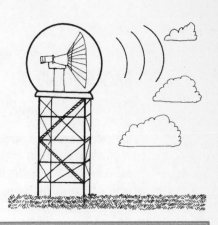

Browse the INFORMATION Web sites (click on the links at the above site) to learn about weather satellites and radar. Use the MAP sites to compare current radar and satellite maps of the United States. Then complete the chart below.

Weather Satellite

How does it work? _____

_____

What is it good at seeing? (circle all that apply)

cloudiness	rain	snow
wind speed	tornadoes	thunderstorms
wind direction	air moisture	temperature of atmosphere

· ·

Weather Radar

How does it work? _____

_____

What is it good at seeing? (circle all that apply)

cloudiness	rain	snow
wind speed	wind direction	thunderstorms
tornadoes	air moisture	temperature of atmosphere

Science
Language Arts

Wild Weather

Students investigate unusual weather phenomena.

BACKGROUND

As sunlight or moonlight passes through Earth's atmosphere, the gases, water molecules, and dust in the air absorb, reflect, refract, diffract, or scatter the light. *Reflection* is when light bounces off an object, while *refraction* is when light bends as it passes through an object. In *diffraction*, light bends as it passes around the edge of an object. These light-altering processes can create weather phenomena such as colorful sunsets, rainbows, glories, halos, parhelia (sun dogs), and sun pillars.

DOING THE ACTIVITY

1. Ask students, Who has seen a rainbow? What causes them? Explain that water and ice in the air can bend, bounce, and scatter light, creating rainbows and other kinds of weather phenomena, such as halos around the sun, sun dogs, glories, and iridescent clouds.

2. Photocopy and distribute page 35 to students or student pairs. Have students click on the links at the above Web site and choose a type of phenomena to explore. Or, you may assign each student one of these six basic atmospheric phenomena: halo, rainbow, glory, sun pillar, parhelia (sundog), or iridescent cloud (iridescence).

3. Have students fill their charts with information from the Web sites.

4. Invite students who are reporting on the same phenomena to meet, compare notes, and prepare a class presentation.

More To Do:

Make a Rainbow

Set a clear container filled with water near a window in direct sunlight. Place a white posterboard between the container and the window. Hold a small mirror in the water facing the sunlight and adjust its angle until a rainbow is cast on the posterboard.

Name(s) _____   Date _____

GO TO: www.scholastic.com/profbooks/netexplorations/index.htm

A Phenomenal Weather Report

Browse the links at the above Web site to find a good picture of the weather phenomenon you chose or your teacher assigned to you. Print it out and paste it on the back of this paper. Then use information on the Web sites to complete the chart below.

1. Name of phenomenon: _____

2. In what part of the sky are you likely to see it? _____

_____

3. When are you likely to see it? During, before, or after what kind of weather? With what kinds of clouds? _____

_____

4. Have you ever seen one? _____

_____

5. When and where? _____

_____

6. Is the sunlight bent, bounced, or scattered? _____

7. How does it happen? _____

_____

_____

Science
Social
Studies
Critical
Thinking

Weather Fact or Folklore?

Students assess the weather sense and science of common weather proverbs.

BACKGROUND

People have been observing wind, rain, cloud, and temperature patterns throughout history in an attempt to predict the weather. All cultures are filled with weather folklore and sayings like "Red sky at night, sailors' delight. Red sky in the morning, sailors take warning." Such sayings are a testament to humankind's interest in weather watching and forecasting. While many of these proverbs are based on fact or observation for some regions in some situations, others are simply superstition.

DOING THE ACTIVITY

1. Ask students what they think this weather proverb means: "Red sky at night, sailors' delight. Red sky in the morning, sailors take warning." *(Seeing a red sky at night means good weather is on the way, while a red sky in the morning means bad weather is on the way.)* Is it true? *(Yes. Fiery red skies occur when light reflects off particles in the air. An extra-red sunset can mean that thin fair-weather cirrus clouds are in the west where most weather comes from, so good weather is on the way. A red sunrise may mean the cirrus clouds in the east are on their way out and storm clouds may be on the way in.)*

2. Photocopy and distribute page 37 to student pairs or small groups. Provide students with scissors so that they can cut out their cards. (Students can also paste their cards onto heavy paper, if desired.)

3. Have students use the links at the above Web site to complete their cards.

4. When students have finished, allow them to compare their findings.

More To Do:

Say What?

Invite students to invent their own weather sayings based on personal experiences and observations. Does a pet behave a certain way before a storm? What does the sky look like before it snows?

Name(s) _____   Date _____

GO TO: www.scholastic.com/profbooks/netexplorations/index.htm

Wise Weather Sayings?

Cut out the four cards below and browse the links at the above Web site to find out about the weather proverbs on each card. Write what you think the proverb means on the front. Then write "weather" or not you think it is true on the back along with why you think so.

1. **Halo 'round the moon, rain's coming soon.**

   What does it mean?

   _____

   _____

   _____

   _____

2. **The higher the clouds, the better the weather.**

   What does it mean?

   _____

   _____

   _____

   _____

3. **Geese fly higher in fair weather than in foul.**

   What does it mean?

   _____

   _____

   _____

   _____

4. **Bushy-tailed squirrels gathering lots of nuts means a hard winter is on the way.**

   What does it mean?

   _____

   _____

   _____

   _____

Science Careers

Weather as Work

Students investigate meteorology as a career and then interview each other for specific meteorology jobs advertised online.

BACKGROUND

Meteorologists measure weather conditions, study storms, and can even be television personalities. Meteorology is a diverse field, but nearly all jobs require at least a bachelor's degree. *Forecasters* are meteorologists who analyze weather maps and information to prepare weather reports, make forecasts, and issue weather warnings for the public or for private businesses. *Research meteorologists* conduct research on how weather works and on forecasting tools and technologies.

DOING THE ACTIVITY

1. Ask students what they think a meteorologist does. Make sure that students understand the breadth of the field of weather science.

2. Photocopy and distribute page 39 to student pairs. Have students browse the INFORMATION links at the above Web site to get basic information about the field of meteorology. Then have them browse the CLASSIFIEDS sites to find two job advertisements to print out: one for a forecaster and one for a researcher.

3. Provide students with scissors and paste so that they can attach their printed-out job advertisements to their worksheets. Students then cut apart the two ads (each with its meteorologist description).

4. Have each student in the pair take one of the ads and write interview questions for the job as if he or she were a recruiter looking to fill the position. Then ask students to interview each other for their respective jobs.

More To Do:

Meet a Meteorologist

Invite a working meteorologist from a local TV station or nearby National Weather Service office to come speak to your class.

Name(s) _____   Date _____

Working for the Weather

Browse the INFORMATION links at the above Web site to learn about the field of meteorology. Then print out two job advertisements from the CLASSIFIEDS sites, one that fits each meteorologist description below, and paste them to this page. Use the ads to interview classmates for the job! Write questions to ask your job seeker on the back of this page.

Research Meteorologist

Meteorology is a science where new discoveries are made each year. Research meteorologists work to invent new and better weather-measuring instruments and to develop better forecasting computers. They also study the basics of how weather works, from what creates a killer tornado to why global warming is happening.

Paste ad here

Forecaster

This kind of meteorologist forecasts the weather and tells people about it. He or she looks at weather maps and other resources to predict the weather, track storms, and prepare weather reports. A forecaster can work for a TV or radio station, a government office like the National Weather Service, the military, or businesses like airlines and farms.

Paste ad here

Science
Art

Stormy Posters

Students create posters about types of storms using pictures and information gathered from Web sites.

BACKGROUND

Disturbances in the atmosphere cause periods of violent weather, or storms. Storms create strong winds and often bring rain, snow, sleet, hail, or other precipitation that is sometimes accompanied by lightning. The main types of storms are thunderstorms, tornadoes, hurricanes, and winter storms. Winter storms include blizzards, ice storms, sleet storms, and northeasters.

DOING THE ACTIVITY

1. Prepare students for the activity by asking the class to name kinds of storms. As students identify types of storms, list them on the board. Once the list is complete, assign each group of students a type of storm, or allow them to choose one.

2. Photocopy and distribute page 41 to each group. Have students click on the links at the above Web site to answer the questions and plan their posters. Note that the INFORMATION sites are general sites about storms. Students will need to follow links to access information about their chosen type of storm.

3. Invite students to print out pictures or diagrams to use on their posters from the INFORMATION and STORM PHOTOS Web sites.

More To Do:

Which Winter Storm?

Winter storms come in a variety of forms, including blizzards, northeasters, and ice storms. Challenge student groups to sort out the differences among winter storms and to write descriptions of each, including the weather conditions that cause them.

GO TO: www.scholastic.com/profbooks/netexplorations/index.htm

Storm Poster Planner

Use the links at the above Web site to learn about the kind of storm you picked. Think about what you'd like to include on your poster. Answer these questions to help you plan your poster.

Facts About _____
(kind of storm)

1. What are they like? _____

2. Where do they happen? _____

3. During what time of year are they common? _____

4. What weather causes them? _____

5. How are they predicted or forecasted? _____

6. What else is interesting about them? _____

7. Plan your poster here. Make sure to include pictures or drawings.

Science
Health
Language
Arts

Storm Safety

Each student group writes a play about how to be prepared and stay safe during a type of storm.

BACKGROUND

Storms can quickly create life-threatening situations. Tornadoes destroy homes, hurricanes and thunderstorms create floods, and winter storms make traveling hazardous. The National Weather Service issues alerts to the public about severe weather. A *watch* means that severe weather is possible within the designated area and that residents should be on alert. A *warning* indicates that severe weather has been reported or is imminent and that all residents should take necessary precautions.

DOING THE ACTIVITY

1. Start a discussion about emergency preparedness at school. Why are regular fire or tornado drills important? How does the public know what to do during storms? What are effective ways to teach people about storm preparedness?

2. Photocopy and distribute page 43 to small groups of students. Tell them that each group will be writing a play to educate the public about what to do to stay safe during a storm.

3. Assign each group one of these severe weather situations: hurricane, tornado, thunderstorm, winter storm, or flood.

4. Have students use the links at the above Web site to learn about the hazards of and safety procedures for their storm. Answering the questions on their sheet will help guide them.

5. When students have finished gathering information, invite them to write their plays away from the computer.

More To Do:

School Storm Plan

Invite an administrator to speak to the class about the school's plan for a tornado, hurricane, or other severe weather event. Discuss the plan to make sure everyone knows what to do.

Name(s) _____   Date _____

GO TO: www.scholastic.com/profbooks/netexplorations/index.htm

Play it Safe During Storms

Knowing how to stay safe during a storm is important. Use the links at the above Web site to gather information about the hazards of your chosen kind of storm and then write a play about being storm-smart.

Storm Safety for _____
                              (type of storm)

1. What dangerous weather do these storms create? (For example, lightning, flooding, strong winds, or cold temperatures.)

_____

2. What makes the weather dangerous to people? (For example, bad road conditions, hypothermia, or collapsing buildings.)

_____

3. When is a "watch" issued for a storm? When is a "warning" issued? How do residents learn if an alert has been issued? Do they have a lot of time to take action?

_____

4. How can people be prepared for this kind of storm? What can they do to keep safe?

_____

Writing Your Play

Title:_____

What is the basic story?_____

Who are the characters?_____

How many scenes are there? _____

Where does each scene take place?_____

Quick & Easy Internet Activities for the One-Computer Classroom: Weather **43**

Science
Critical
Thinking

Looking at Lightning

Students learn about lightning's destructive power and then design a lightning-proof building.

BACKGROUND

Lightning occurs when electricity travels between negatively and positively charged parts of a cloud during a thunderstorm. When a cloud discharges and lightning flashes, it can heat up the air as much as 50,000°F along its path. A bolt of lightning delivers thousands to millions of volts of electricity—enough to light up a town. Lightning can cause damage to trees, homes, and vulnerable electrical equipment. It can also kill.

DOING THE ACTIVITY

1. Ask students what they know about lightning safety. Assess what they know about how lightning occurs, what attracts it, and what kind of damage it can cause.

2. Photocopy and distribute page 45 to each student or student pair. Tell them that they will be designing a lightning-proof building.

3. Have students browse the links at the above Web site to learn or review lightning basics. Have them answer the questions on the worksheet to focus their thinking. (Consider reviewing the answers with students before they design their buildings.)

4. When all students have finished their designs, allow them to gather in groups and design an improved building by combining ideas.

More To Do:

Lightning Mini-Bolts

On a low-humidity day, students can make tiny lightning bolts. Have students blow up a balloon and tie it closed. Have them rub the balloon on their hair or a wool glove. Tell students to hold a metal paper clip in one hand and slowly move it toward the balloon until it touches. They will hear a crackling sound—a discharge of static electricity that's like a tiny clap of thunder. (Students will be able to see the sparks in a very dark room.)

Name(s) _____   Date _____

GO TO: www.scholastic.com/profbooks/netexplorations/index.htm

Lightning-Resistant Building

Browse the links at the above Web site to learn about the awesome power of lightning and think about what makes a building at risk for lightning strikes. Take notes by answering the questions below and then design a building that is safe from lightning.

Think About Lightning

1. What causes lightning?_____

2. When does it happen? _____

3. What kinds of materials attract lightning? _____

4. What can lightning damage? _____

5. What is a lightning rod? _____

6. What are some things people can do to make their homes lightning-proof? _____

_____

7. Design your lightning-proof house, office, or school here. Label the different features.

Science
Math
Geography

Tracking a Hurricane

Students use real data to track the path of Hurricane Floyd.

BACKGROUND

A *tropical storm* officially becomes a *hurricane* when its winds reach speeds of more than 74 miles per hour. Meteorologists, as well as many amateur weather watchers, track the paths of tropical storms as they develop into hurricanes. Following and plotting a storm's path as it develops and moves is how scientists forecast its strength and predict its direction. It's also what evacuation plans are based on.

DOING THE ACTIVITY

1. Photocopy and distribute page 47 to students along with a copy of a tracking map from a MAP Web site (click on the links at the above site), or allow students to print out their own maps. Make sure students understand how to read the map by reviewing longitude and latitude. Check for understanding by challenging students to find sample position points.

2. Have students use the longitude and latitude data points on their charts on page 47 to plot the path of 1999's Hurricane Floyd.

3. Once students have finished their hurricane tracking paths, invite them to go to the FLOYD TRACKS Web sites and compare them to other Floyd tracks.

More To Do:

Rate It

Investigate the Saffir-Simpson scale for rating hurricanes. Then rate Hurricane Floyd's strength at each plot point on the chart on page 47.

Name(s) _____   Date _____

GO TO: www.scholastic.com/profbooks/netexplorations/index.htm

Following Hurricane Floyd

Use the longitude and latitude numbers in the chart below to create plot points on your map for every 12 hours of Hurricane Floyd. Connect the points to see Floyd's destructive path. Then visit the FLOYD TRACKS Web sites (click on the links at the above site) to compare your plotted path to those of others. How do they compare?

Day/ Time	Latitude (°N)	Longitude (°W)	Wind (mph)	Tropical Storm (39–74 mph) Hurricane (75 mph or more)
9 Sept/12 A.M.	16.7	52.6	52	tropical storm
9 Sept/12 P.M.	17.3	55.1	58	tropical storm
10 Sept/12 A.M.	18.3	57.2	69	tropical storm
10 Sept/12 P.M.	19.3	58.8	81	hurricane
11 Sept/12 A.M.	20.8	60.4	92	hurricane
11 Sept/12 P.M.	21.9	62.0	109	hurricane
12 Sept/12 A.M.	22.7	64.1	98	hurricane
12 Sept/12 P.M.	23.0	66.2	121	hurricane
13 Sept/12 A.M.	23.4	68.7	144	hurricane
13 Sept/12 P.M.	23.9	71.4	155	hurricane
14 Sept/12 A.M.	24.5	74.0	132	hurricane
14 Sept/12 P.M.	25.4	76.3	121	hurricane
15 Sept/12 A.M.	27.1	77.7	132	hurricane
15 Sept/12 P.M.	29.3	78.9	115	hurricane
16 Sept/12 A.M.	32.1	78.7	104	hurricane
16 Sept/12 P.M.	35.7	76.8	81	hurricane
17 Sept/12 A.M.	40.6	73.5	58	tropical storm or extratropical storm
17 Sept/12 P.M.	43.3	70.6	52	tropical storm or extratropical storm

Resources

Books, ⊙ Software, Videos, and Web sites about Weather.

Teacher Resources

The Weather Book (USA Today)
by Jack Williams (Vintage Books, 1997).
All the weather basics explained with *USA Today*'s trademark graphics by its "Ask Jack" meteorologist.

The Wow's & Why's of Weather
by Mary Kay Carson (Scholastic, 2000). A teaching resource packed with information, activities, and reproducible pages about storm science, cool weather careers, and more.

How the Weather Works
by Michael Allaby (Reader's Digest, 1999). This book includes more than 1,000 color illustrations and photos showing weather principles, step-by-step experiments, and weather-instrument building instructions.

Weather
by Janice VanCleave (Wiley, 1995). The subtitle, "Mind-Boggling Experiments You Can Turn Into Science Fair Projects," says it all!

It's Raining Cats and Dogs
by Franklyn M. Branley (Houghton Mifflin, 1987). A fun book filled with weather facts and folklore, experiments, and explanations of weather events.

Eyewitness: Weather
(Eyewitness, 1996). Fabulous information and graphics guide students through a fun exploration of wind, rain, hail, and more.

USA Today Weather Page
www.usatoday.com/weather

The Weather World 2010 Project
ww2010.atmos.uiuc.edu

The Weather Channel
www.weather.com

Student Resources

Everything Weather
(Weather Channel, 1996). This multimedia research tool allows students to investigate all aspects of weather, view fascinating videos and photographs, and access interactive weather maps. Includes a Teacher's Guide.

Weather Forecasting
by Gail Gibbons (Aladdin, 1993). The easy-to-read text and colorful illustrations in this behind-the-scenes look at a modern weather station answer basic questions about weather forecasting.

Chinook!
by Michael O. Tunnell (Tambourine Books, 1993). A brother and sister meet an old man who tells them tales of the warm winter winds called *chinooks*.

The Cloud Book
by Tomie de Paola (Holiday House, 1985). The ten most common types of clouds are introduced, as well as the myths inspired by their shapes and what they foretell about the weather.

Play Time for Kids
(National Weather Service)
www.nws.noaa.gov/om/reachout/kidspage.shtm

The Franklin Institute Online: Weather
www.fi.edu/weather

Weatherland
www.earthstation.com